Boise State University Western Writers Series   Number 76

John Gregory Dunne

By Mark Royden Winchell

Clemson University

Editors: Wayne Chatterton
James H. Maguire

Business Manager:
James Hadden

Cover Design and Illustration
by Arny Skov, Copyright 1986

Boise State University, Boise, Idaho

Library of Congress Card No. 86-70655

International Standard Book No. 0-88430-075-7

Printed in the United States of America by
Boise State University Printing and Graphics Services
Boise, Idaho

John Gregory Dunne

John Gregory Dunne

In the January 1981 issue of *Horizon*, John Lahr writes: "California is a state of amateur outdoorsmen—of runners, of swimmers, of bikers, of sailors, and of golfers. Here, the surface of life can be enjoyed without analysis. Amidst the sun, surf, and caesar salads, intellectual stimulation is never a high priority." He goes on to trash those who "never question the consequences of Los Angeles or the California scene . . . —the general absence of community, the moral stupor, the greedy self-aggrandizement, and the emotional impoverishment that characterize and enchant the place" ("Entrepreneurs" 39). These comments, so typical of a certain anti-California mentality, would scarcely be worth our notice except that they are contained in a particularly mean-spirited attack on two of the most prominent writers of the contemporary American West—Joan Didion and John Gregory Dunne. Because of Didion's heritage as a fifth-generation Californian, her identity as a Western writer is generally conceded and has been frequently discussed. Transplanted from the East, Dunne's roots do not go as deep as hers, but he compensates by writing with a convert's zeal about his adopted home. Since an examination of Dunne as a naturalized Westerner is long overdue, let us leave the moral posturings of John Lahr to see what all the fuss is about.

Dunne's original home was Hartford, Connecticut, where he was born on 25 May 1932, the fifth of six children of Richard Edward and Dorothy Burns Dunne. His maternal grandfather had "arrived in this country a few years after the Civil War, an unlettered child of twelve out from belowdecks and the ould sod, a placard around his neck on which was scrawled his name to identify him to his American relatives" (*Vegas* 97-98). Over the next seventy years he became a prosperous grocer and banker in Frog Hollow, the city's Irish ghetto and died "rich and revered, as the *Luftwaffe* was blitzing London" (*Vegas* 98). As the product of a family that "went from steerage to suburbia in three generations" (*Vegas* 97), Dunne is particularly sensitive to the rich literary possibilities of depicting ethnic culture in the process of assimilation, something he has called the "mother lode" of his muse. The other formative influence on his vocation as a writer was his childhood stutter. To offset this disability, he developed a knack for expressing himself on paper and for listening to the speech of others.

In *Vegas: A Memoir of a Dark Season* (1974), Dunne writes: "Except for the occasional wedding or christening or funeral, it is nearly twenty years now since I voluntarily entered a church to help celebrate the sacrament of the Mass, yet the Catholicism of my childhood remains the one salient fact of my life" (92). Not only is this cultural background reflected in his two novels, *True Confessions* (1977) and *Dutch Shea, Jr.* (1982), but it permeates an entire autobiographical section of *Vegas*. Here, Dunne recalls being sent to Portsmouth Priory, an elite Rhode Island boarding school run by Benedictine monks, after his mother had discovered a hoard of forty-nine dozen prophylactics, which he had stolen as a fringe benefit of his job with a wholesale drug company.

One of the favorite ways of hazing new students at the Priory was to persuade them that the founder of the school, Father Hugh, was notorious for giving easy penances. When a newcomer entered Father Hugh's confessional, the older boys would "huddle outside the box and listen, trying to stifle their laughter."

"Bless me, Father, for I have sinned ... " "WHAT'S THAT LAD?" Father Hugh's voice would thunder from the confessional. He was by then so deaf that he had to shout to hear the sound of his own words. "MASTUR-BATION, IS THAT WHAT YOU SAID?"

"Their shame was so intense," Dunne recalls, "that some of the younger boys would actuallly refuse to come out of the confessional. Others would emerge in tears. No one ever confessed to Father Hugh more than once" (100-01).

Like so many lapsed Catholics, Dunne finds that some of his most vivid and humorous memories are of childhood autoeroticism, a fact that surely has something to do with the moral imperative to confess that particular sin. He therefore tells us, in hilarious detail, about the solicitude of Eddie Toomey, who in the seventh grade taught Dunne how to masturbate—an art that he perfected over the years until, four days before his twenty-first birthday, he lost his virginity. Upon Eddie Toomey's sage advice, Dunne would always enhance his pleasure by "thinking of someone": June Haver, Joan Fontaine, Jeanne Crain, and—preeminently—Terry Moore, a colorchrome picture of whom he had clipped from the cover of the *New York News's* Sunday supplement and pinned to the back of his door in college. Dunne recalls being "mortified years later when I discovered that the son of one of these inspirations was in the same nursery school as my daughter. 'How do you do?' she said at the Christmas pageant. I almost said, 'We've met' " (90). What we have here is an Irish Catholic version of Philip Roth's Alexander Portnoy, with the Virgin Mary as the ultimate Jewish mother.

To this day Dunne harbors fond memories of the legendary pros-titute Phyl Coker, who introduced him to the mysteries of sex when he was an undergraduate at Princeton. Indeed, Phyl Coker introduced several generations of Princeton undergraduates to the mysteries of sex. Once when Dunne was serving as a bartender at reunion weekend, a drunken member of the class of '35 asked him if he had ever known the Coker sisters. In every way possible, Dunne assured him. And the man replied: "Phyl Coker was my first piece of ass" (104). That was the fall of the alum's freshman year, 1931. The young bartender thinks: "Hoover was president, Franklin Roosevelt was in Albany, Hindenburg and the Weimar Republic were still afloat, the dollar was not, and I had not even been born" (104). Some seventeen years later, Dunne was in New York for a brief stay and called Phyl Coker one afternoon "to find where the years had gone and what they had meant." "But Jesus, darling," she said, "I'm sixty-two years old" (108).

Graduating from Princeton in 1954, Dunne spent two years in the U.S. Army, before settling in New York, where he worked first for an advertising agency and a major trade magazine, and then—for five years—as a staff writer with *Time*. Also, during the early sixties, he was at least peripherally connected with William F. Buckley, Jr.—who published his first free-lance piece—and the brilliant young writers—John Leonard, Garry Wills, Arlene Croce, Renata Adler, and others—then contributing to *National Review*. Of these, the two who have had the most significant impact on his career are Noel E. Parmental, Jr., and Joan Didion.

Dunne thought enough of Parmental to dedicate *Vegas* to him, but by the time he published *Quintana & Friends* four years later, they were no longer speaking. Nevertheless, in the introduction to that volume, he refers to Parmental—whom he does not mention by name, presumably on the assumption that those who don't know wouldn't understand if you told them—as being "as close to a mentor as anyone I have ever known" (xviii). "I ranged over New

York with him," Dunne recalls, "picking up his lessons by osmosis, Sancho Panza to his demented knight. I met the Gallos and the widow of the celery king of the Harlem Market. I went to VID [Village Independent Democrats] meetings in the Village with him, and Lexington Avenue Democratic Club parties; he would insult the VID and the Lexington Avenue Democrats, disrupt their events and push off into the night .... His idea of high good humor was to send a right-wing dialectician, who had abandoned both Judaism and the Communist Party for the Right and Anglo-Catholicism, an Episcopalian hymnal" (xviii-xix).

Joan Didion and John Gregory Dunne met on opposite halves of a double date. When his girl made a major, if entirely fortuitous, contribution to literary history by passing out drunk in Didion's apartment, Joan fixed rice and red beans and she and John stayed up talking all night. They remained only friends for six years until 1963, when they had lunch one day to discuss the manuscript of her first novel, *Run River*. Shortly thereafter they moved into an apartment together and, a year later, were married. In April 1964 they took tentative leaves from their jobs to visit southern California and have remained there ever since.

Despite a lean first year in which they earned $7,000 between them, Didion and Dunne began to establish themselves as accomplished free-lance journalists and bought successive homes with their earnings from screenwriting. Their film credits include *The Panic in Needle Park* (1971), the 1976 remake of *A Star Is Born* (starring Barbra Streisand), on which they made a small fortune although they left the picture before it was completed, and film versions of her *Play It as It Lays* (1972) and his *True Confessions* (1981). In 1982, Dunne reckoned that their marriage had consisted of "15 years of good days and three years of bad days, ... a terrific ratio" (Kasindorf 18). If their readers are surprised by the relative

9

stability of their marriage, that is because the two authors have not hesitated to write about the bad moments. As Dunne puts it: "Life is difficult enough without having to try to find material" (Kasindorf 15). One ready-made source of material upon which Didion and Dunne have consistently drawn is the experience of raising Quintana, the infant daughter whom they adopted in 1966.

Dunne and Didion are such devoted parents that reading descriptions of life with Quintana is somewhat like watching home movies, something that I have come to appreciate more since becoming an uncle. Indeed, a picture of the child—in sunbonnet and tennis shoes, with legs crossed, hands clasped, and sun glasses at her feet—stares at us from the jacket of Dunne's 1978 collection of essays, *Quintana & Friends*. The initial selection in this volume, a witty and affectionate account of the adoption of Quintana and of the challenges faced by adoptive parents, was originally published in *Esquire* at about the same time that *Roots* was causing such a national sensation. One of the main sociological points that comes across here is the extent to which attitudes toward the rights of adopted children have become more enlightened since the days of radio soap opera. Alluding to the more recent television soap opera *Upstairs-Downstairs*, Dunne lets us know that he and his wife are not "Hudson and Mrs. Bridges, below-stairs surrogates taking care of the wee one" (7).

The wee one herself is depicted as a charming and precocious young tyke who is so much a part of her parents' professional lives that Dunne even discussed this essay with her to see if she would be embarrassed by it. Once when an actress received an award for a picture that the Dunnes had written for her, the actress's acceptance speech "drove Quintana into an absolute fury. 'She never,' Quintana reported, 'thanked *us*'" (6). With the prepubescent cunning of a female Tom Sawyer, she has even turned the sow's ear of adoption into a silk purse. At a party with twenty other little girls who were discussing the gynecological specifics of birth, Quintana announced that she had not emerged from that mundane orifice, but had been adopted. "[S]he pulled it off with such élan and aplomb that in moments the other children were bemoaning their own misfortune in not being adopted, one even claiming, 'Well I was almost adopted' " (6).

Dunne's literary career was launched during a time of profound change in American letters. The hegemony enjoyed by the realistic novel from the time of Mark Twain and William Dean Howells until just after the Second World War was coming under assault from a younger generation of writers who were greatly influenced by the neo-fabulism of avant-garde European and Latin American fiction, principally by the work of Franz Kafka. Along with the rise of this new literary movement—generally referred to as post-modernism—came a fundamental change in the reading public itself. The bourgeois audience that had always been the primary market for mimetic fiction was now turning to more technologically advanced storytelling media, such as films and television, or to pulp fantasy—spy thrillers, horror stories, Harlequin romances, and pornography. Thus, a writer such as John Gregory Dunne, who by training and temperament probably should have begun his career as a realistic novelist, turned his considerable talents to feature journalism.

To date, four of Dunne's six published books could be classified as highly literate non-fiction. The most recent of these—*Quintana & Friends* (1978)—is a collection of short pieces written over a period of nearly two decades. These include selections from regular columns that he shared with Didion in the *Saturday Evening Post*—1967 to 1969—and *Esquire*—1976 to 1977. His first three books, however, are full-length non-fiction narratives which reflect a rather pronounced evolution in style from conventional journalism to the type of personal memoir that made his later fictions (*True Confessions* and *Dutch Shea, Jr.*) possible. The first of these was *Delano: The Story of the California Grape Strike* (1967).

If nothing else, *Delano* is a tribute to Dunne's journalistic prescience. In 1965 he peddled all over New York the idea of doing a story on the farm worker's strike and was turned down everywhere: " 'Who the hell has ever heard of Cesar Chavez?' asked one editor who has since nominated him for sainthood" (*Quintana* 13). Dunne finally sold the idea to the *Saturday Evening Post* and managed to scoop just about every other national journalist in reporting on what would become a *cause célèbre* of the late sixties. Precisely because of the political volatility of the situation, it was difficult for most people writing about it to maintain any sense of objectivity. As Dunne would later observe: "A man with thousands of acres worth millions of dollars simply did not have the emotional appeal of a faceless crowd of brown-skinned men, women and children eking out a fetid existence, crammed into substandard housing, isolated by language and custom from a community that scorned them. Never mind that the grower was mortgaged to the eyeballs.... [H]igh interest rates did not sing like food stamps" (*Quintana* 124).

Despite Dunne's objectivity, one can draw certain inferences about his attitude toward the situation in Delano. For one thing, he depicts the struggle between the growers and the workers as a Faulknerian drama of social change. He cannot caricature the growers as west-coast Simon Legrees when he found several of them to be personally congenial and probably had more in common with them than with Chavez's troops, Dunne's Central Valley wife being more Sartoris than Snopes. Moreover, one detects a certain impatience with the radical chic of some of Chavez's Anglo followers. The growers appear less greedy than stubborn, hostile not to their workers but to the concept of change itself. There was no question that Chavez's insistence on decent treatment and living wages for his people was the morally superior position and that the growers' crude policy of red-baiting was very much beside the point. But the hard economic reality of the situation was that human labor was cheaper than mechanization only so long as the labor was exploited. As Chavez proceeded to win his battles, he was simultaneously losing his war.

Because Dunne's book was completed while the grape strike was still in progress and updated while the lettuce boycott was just getting underway, it is less than conclusive about the ultimate impact of Cesar Chavez on American society. In any event, Dunne is not the sort of writer we would go to for such an assessment. Although he is an intelligent social commentator and has done his homework by reading the historical writings of Carey McWilliams, Dunne is most adept at setting the mood or sketching the background of a situation. It is perhaps easier to do this by focusing on peripheral rather than central players in a historical drama. Consequently, *Delano* gives us very little insight into Chavez while vividly evoking the atmosphere of the strike with dozens of suggestive vignettes. For example, in describing the office of the farmworker's union, he writes: "One day I came upon a hefty Mexican woman, with most of her teeth missing, engrossed in a *Coed* [magazine] article entitled 'How to Act on a Double Date' and containing such instructions as: 'Bring your coat to the table. Tipping is expensive'" (13).

Dunne is also good at depicting the slightly patronizing attitude of inveterate crusaders who had latched on to the Chavez movement. He remembers, in particular, talking with a comely "redheaded girl in her mid-twenties who had previously been in Mississippi with SNCC. She seemed to accept the fact that the Mexicans would one day no longer need her, as the Negroes no longer wanted her in the South. I wondered what she would do when she was older and disenchantment had set in. And then she said, 'Maybe I'll organize the middle class' " (120-21). There was also the time that a doctor who was generously donating his services to the workers was called to see a sick baby and asked the parents to turn on the light in the bedroom so that he could see the infant. What he did not realize was that "the only functioning light bulb in the entire house was hung from a wire in the kitchen" (99).

If Cesar Chavez is a vague and ill-defined presence in this book, Chavez's mentor, the free-lance radical Saul Alinsky, is not. Although he was known to the people in the Valley only as someone who's "got a name like a bomb thrower" (112), Alinsky was Dunne's kind of guy—ironic, plainspoken, and "totally without illusions" (53). " 'Wherever I go there's trouble,' he said as he stirred a Scotch on the rocks with his finger. 'I've always said that the only way to talk to the Establishment is not through their ears but through their rears. You've got to shaft them up the ass. Liberals would never talk like that' " (53-54).

Alinsky's main complaint about the farmworker's movement is that there is nothing to sustain it after the fad has worn off and the political groupies have moved on to a sexier cause. Had Alinsky been running the show, he would have sought a patron to under-write the union. "I would have gone to Hoffa," he tells Dunne. "I would have said 'Listen, everyone thinks you're nothing but a goddam hoodlum. You need to pretty yourself up. And the way to do it is to help the poor migrant Mexican.' Jesus, he needed something. But now he's in the can" (171).

In "Memento Delano," a piece published in *Atlantic Monthly* in 1971 and reprinted in both a second edition of *Delano* and in *Quintana & Friends*, Dunne finds a more personal narrative voice by recalling some of his most vivid memories of 1967. "I remember a cool night in the foothills of the Sierra," he tells us, "when a panicky young farm worker was casually seduced by a California golden girl. I remember the boy still desperately picking on his guitar even as he was being led off to the bedroom and I remember that the next morning when the girl knocked on my door to wake me up she wasn't wearing any clothes." Then, shifting the scene, he writes: "I remember a grower named Jack Pandol, whom I liked personally better than anyone I met in Delano, telling me that he really had very little in common with his brother-in-law, who was also a farmer, and when I asked why, he said simply, 'He's in alfalfa, I'm in grapes'" (*Quintana* 116).

More conventional journalists would have ignored these two seemingly trivial incidents; however, to Dunne they speak volumes. On the one hand, there is the chasm in social and sexual custom which divides the *campesinos* from their slumming affluent allies in a way that no amount of political good faith can bridge. On the other hand, there is the grower's "sense of being alone, of embattlement, the feeling that if he didn't have much in common with his brother-in-law, he was going to have even less in common with Chavez" (117). What ties these incidents together is Dunne's presence as observer, a fact emphasized by the oft-repeated refrain "I remember."

At the end of "Memento Delano," Dunne attempts to assess Chavez's historical significance by commenting on his role in shaping the ethnic consciousness of young Hispanics. Although Chavez operated in the vineyards, Dunne believes his principal influence to have been on the young people in the barrios. Having "deserted the hoe for the car wash" (131), these young people were in need of a role model. In their neighborhoods, one could see "whitewashed on fences and abandoned storefronts, the paint splattered and uneven, signs painted on the run in the dark of night, '*Es mejor morir de pie que vivir de rodillas*'—'Better to die standing that to live on your knees.' The words are those of Emiliano Zapata, but the spirit that wrote them there was fired by Cesar Chavez" (131).

When judged by ordinary standards of journalism, *Delano* is a first-rate piece of reportage. To call it "new journalism," however, is to invite a comparison with the contemporaneous work of Capote, Wolfe, Mailer, and others, not the least of whom was Joan Didion herself. When seen in that light, and in comparison with Dunne's later work, the virtues of *Delano* seem like drawbacks. There is perhaps too much journalistic exposition and too little development through the novelistic devices of setting, characterization, and dialogue. The impact of Dunne's experience as a staff writer at *Time* is evident, even down to his telling us—on p. 9—that Delano is "pronouonced De*layn*o." If "Memento Delano" seems more in the tradition of the creative non-fiction that dominated the highbrow magazine market in the late sixties and early seventies, it may be that during the crucial years from 1967 to 1971 Dunne was developing greater confidence in himself as a stylist. Those were the years of his *Saturday Evening Post* column and his brilliant second book, *The Studio* (1969).

In order to understand Dunne's contribution to the literature of Hollywood, of which *The Studio* is the prime example, we must remember that for the past fifty years two exaggerated images of the film capital have dominated our national psyche. For millions of Americans, Hollywood is the realization of the American Dream, a far-off enchanted city where a lucky few can rise not only from rags to riches but from obscurity to fame. For many others, it is less El Dorado than a fool's paradise. The image of what Didion and Dunne call "Hollywood the Destroyer," epitome of everything that is venal and meretricious in American life, is as much an article of faith for highbrow cynics as the original myth of the heavenly city is for the naive of middle America. Anyone who has ever read a "Hollywood novel"—by the disillusioned writers who came west for big bucks with the introduction of sound into motion pictures in the thirties and remained to debunk the scam that fed them—knows that just as every thesis produces an antithesis, so too does every myth generate an anti-myth.

The great offense that Dunne and other recent revisionists, including Didion, have committed against our national pieties is to seek a middle ground between the myth and the anti-myth. The new realism that Dunne represents essentially seeks to *demythologize* Hollywood, to see it as neither Heaven nor Hell, but as a company town where real people live and work. What is involved is something of a dialectical process which results in a kind of anti-anti-myth. Such a point of view lends itself very well to the "objectivity" of journalism. In *The Studio* Dunne takes us inside Twentieth Century Fox and shows us the actual social dynamics of film production and promotion. Eschewing the conventional reportorial techniques used in *Delano*, Dunne relies almost exclusively on description and dialogue—with very little explication—to give us a *cinéma vérité* look at the "real" Hollywood.

The film capital is a place where the Peter Principle is very much at work. "You fail upward here," a young agent tells Dunne. "A guy makes a ten-million-dollar bomb, the big thing is not that he's made a bomb, but that he put together a ten-million-dollar picture .... The worst thing that can happen to you is to have a small success" (100). It is a place where a $500,000-a-year producer can run into his mother, a television extra, on the lot at Desilu. It is a place where a former child star—Jackie Cooper, who has risen to the head of a film company, Screen Gems—can announce that he is having *A Christmas Carol* rewritten because "Dickens was a terrible writer." "In the original, Scrooge is mean and stingy, but you never know why. We're giving him a mother and father, an unhappy childhood, a whole background which will motivate him" (215). And it is a place where the girl friend of a wealthy producer can leave an expensive restaurant with a silver service plate concealed in her tights, for the thrill of the chase, and the headwaiter, pretending not to notice, will add the cost of the plate to the studio's bill.

Although Dunne gives us a broad survey of life at Twentieth Century Fox, the project that particularly captures his imagination is the $18,000,000 extravaganza *Dr. Dolittle*. Flush with the phenomenal success of *The Sound of Music*, the studio is intent on milking the family musical for all that it is worth. With a familiar story, a star-studded cast—e.g., Rex Harrison, Samantha Eggar, Anthony Newley, and Richard Attenborough—and an original score by Leslie Bricusse, *Dr. Dolittle* seems like a sure-fire hit; however, the promotional department at Fox is committed to leaving nothing to chance. Among the list of ten ideas for "special exploitation" of the film, some of the more exotic are: "5. DISCUSS: Local Boards of Education to declare DOCTOR DOLITTLE DAY and release children from school .... 8. Explore DOLITTLE figure in Madame Tussaud's Waxworks in both London and Los Angeles. 9. Explore special citation from Congressional Record. 10. Discuss Vatican screening" (171, 172). And, as a special publicity gimmick, it had been decided that several of the film's animal stars would arrive at the premiere in chauffeured limousines.

The chapter from *The Studio* that Dunne later included in *Quintana & Friends* describes the disastrous sneak preview of *Dr. Dolittle* in Minneapolis. Here, Dunne is most adept at using the Hemingway iceberg technique of letting events speak for themselves with minimal interpretation. For one thing, frequent off-hand references to *The Sound of Music*, which had also been "sneaked" in Minneapolis, remind us of the standard against which the studio is measuring its new effort. Early on, we learn that Rex Harrison—star of *Dr. Dolittle*—has backed out of an agreement to do a remake of *Goodbye, Mr. Chips* for Arthur Jacobs, producer of *Dr. Dolittle*. The subtle implication is that Harrison already realizes that he has done one Jacobs bomb and is not eager for an encore.

When the brass from Fox arrive in Minneapolis, a procession that studio executive Perry Lieber treated—and seemed to equate with—"the annual pilgrimage of the English royal family from Buckingham Palace to Balmoral" (190), everything seems to go wrong. Since the newspaper ad had not mentioned what movie was being shown, the ideal *Dolittle* audience of kids accompanied by their grandparents was not present, but only what theater owner Ted Mann calls "your typically sophisticated Friday night Minneapolis audience" (199). When the people enter the theater they encounter a display for *Camelot* in the lobby, and when the show starts the first thing they see is Rex Harrison riding a giraffe. At the post-preview party, there is much strained frivolity and a plethora of excuses for the tepid reaction to the film. By 1:30 the party is over and the celebrants have cleared out of studio vice-president Richard Zanuck's suite. At four A.M., Zanuck calls his executive assistant Harry Sokolov and tells him to round up three other Fox executives (Stanley Hough, Owen McLean, and David Brown). They convene in Zanuck's suite at 4:45 A.M., and, for the next hour, go over the picture reel by reel. In his pointed final sentence, Dunne tells us: "Arthur Jacobs was not present at this meeting" (203).

At the outset of his book, Dunne explains that he had decided to spend a year at Fox because of his fascination with the extent

19

to which popular media shape the American psyche. "By adolescence," he notes, "children have been programmed with a set of responses and life lessons learned almost totally from motion pictures, television and the recording industry" (7). To understand "something of the state of mind called Hollywood" (9) is also to discover a good deal about what Robert Sklar has dubbed "movie-made America." What Dunne learns during his year at Fox is that "the point of the Studio is the Product" (254).

The most important Product at Fox during Dunne's stay had been *Dr. Dolittle*, and so his narrative concludes—as *A Star Is Born* and *The Day of the Locust* had—with a film premiere:

> Limousines were strung out along Hollywood Boulevard and a police line held back a crowd of hundreds straining to see the 1,400 guests who swept into the theater in jewels and evening dress. Governor and Mrs. Ronald Reagan were there as the guests of Richard Zanuck, and Sophie the Seal disembarked from her limousine wearing a diamond necklace. She was accompanied by Jip the Dog, who was wearing a jeweled collar. Gub-Gub the Pig wore a sequined harness and Chee-Chee the Chimp was in white tie and tails with a top hat and white carnation. (254)

It was a good year for animals at Fox. However, the studio's most successful picture was not *Dr. Dolittle*, but a relatively low-budget, non-hyped production called *Planet of the Apes*.

Of course, Dunne is not just an observer of Hollywood, but also a practicing screenwriter who has no illusions about the literary grandeur of that profession. When *Atlantic* editor Robert Manning asked him why he writes for the movies, Dunne replied: "Because the money is good. Because doing a screenplay is like doing a combination jigsaw-and-crossword puzzle; it's not writing, but it can be fun. And because the other night, after a screening, we went out to a party with Mike Nichols and Candice Bergen and Warren Beatty and Barbra Streisand. I never did that at *Time*" (*Quintana* 189-90). This admission was enough to cause John Lahr to brand Dunne "a groupie by nature and a hustler at heart" (38); a description that Dunne would probably accept as an unintended compliment.

The exchange with Manning was in regard to a candid episodic piece that Dunne had written about his experiences as a screenwriter. This piece (which is self-mockingly called "Tinsel") is written in much the same vein as *The Studio*, except that Dunne and Didion themselves figure prominently in the action. Here, we learn that the aspiring screenwriter should study "the bad movies of good directors . . . [because] in each there is a moment or sequence that stands out in such bold relief from the surrounding debris as to make the reasons for its effectiveness clear" (174). Also, we learn that the most detailed film treatments are less likely to sell an idea for a picture than is a single evocative, and preferably deceptive, line. The one that sold *The Panic in Needle Park* to Joseph Levine was "Romeo and Juliet on junk." A few years later, when the Dunnes wanted to do a film on the music industry, the magic tagline was "James Taylor and Carly Simon in a rock-and-roll version of *A Star Is Born*" (*Quintana* 158).

By the time the movie in question was actually made, it starred Barbra Streisand and Kris Kristofferson and the Dunnes were no longer associated it. Nevertheless, Dunne's account of his relationship with the project, in an essay called "Gone Hollywood," tells us a good deal about the way the film business operates. Although Dunne maintains that neither he nor Didion had ever seen any of the earlier versions of *A Star Is Born*, the only way

21

they could get a studio to underwrite a screenplay about rock performers "was to dress it up in what they perceived as an old but very well-cut suit of clothes." In a line worthy of Sammy Glick himself, Dunne writes: "As long as there was a superficial resemblance to that classic story we had never seen, we would not be in breech of contract" (*Quintana* 159). It is also interesting to note that at the time this idea was conceived, in 1973, Carly Simon's star was rising, while that of her husband James Taylor was falling—having actors play characters similar to themselves is the sort of trope that Billy Wilder used so brilliantly in his 1950 film about Hollywood, *Sunset Boulevard*. When Dunne first approached an executive at Warner Brothers with his idea, the executive replied: "Don't worry about James if you don't use him, we can always find something for him to do, maybe a house in Malibu" (*Quintana* 159).

Although much of the humor in Dunne's writing about Hollywood, especially in *The Studio* and "Tinsel," is at the expense of industry moguls, he is careful to distance himself from the anti-Hollywood crowd. In "Tinsel," for example, he defends the Academy Awards against the condescension of elitist critics such as Andrew Sarris and Vincent Canby, and elsewhere he has devoted an entire essay to attacking Pauline Kael. According to Dunne, the awards are no different from those of any union in any company town. He goes on to speculate that "if the New York film critics, most of whom work for union organized publications, opened their membership to several thousand typesetters from the Typographical Union and projectionists from IATSE and secretaries from the Newspaper Guild, I suspect that the Academy's choices would seem a lot less moribund" (182). In "Gone Hollywood," he sneers at "the dreary cineasts who spend every waking hour in a darkened theater, emerging only to write about The Film in a language said to be

English" (161). Finally, in a more recent piece in the *New York Review of Books*, he even ridicules those who regard "film" as a more highbrow term than "picture" or "movie": " 'Would you call a book a "readie?" ' an adherent of 'film' once asked, as if this were a telling thrust. No, but I wouldn't call a book a sabago stock, sixty-pound weight, either" ("Hessians" 34).

As valuable as his writing about Hollywood continues to be—and even John Simon, who is one of Dunne's frequent targets, says that he "often writes perceptively and elegantly about film" (*Paradigms* 138)—his major contribution to contemporary literature (at least to date) lies in novels that are as far removed from the jacuzzi culture of southern California as the beaches of Malibu are from the fields of Delano. The personal and artistic watershed that transformed the cosmopolitan journalist of the late sixties into the Irish-Catholic novelist of today is documented in his strange third book, *Vegas: A Memoir of a Dark Season*. Here, for the first time, Dunne sheds his reporter's anonymity and becomes his own protagonist, telling us what Las Vegas meant to him at a particular point in his life.

Before the narrative even begins, Dunne writes: *"This is a fiction which recalls a time both real and imagined"*; and the first line of text reads: "In the summer of my nervous breakdown, I went to live in Las Vegas, Clark County, Nevada" (10). There are hints of marital stress throughout the book. Speaking of his home life prior to the departure for Vegas, Dunne tells us: "I sometimes had the feeling that we went from crisis to crisis like old repertory actors going from town to town, every crisis an opening night with new depths to plumb in the performance" (16). One night his wife—whom he never mentions by name—complains of a headache she got from reading a cookbook: "the particular rhythm of the sentences ... upset my alpha waves" (17).

23

Throughout his stay in Vegas, Dunne would call home to share notes with his wife, who characteristically helped him edit the book when he was finished with it. On one such occasion he learned that she was lonely and depressed and that the septic tank had overflowed.

> There was a crash pad next door and one of the couples had taken to boffing on the grass in clear view of our daughter's bedroom window .... The maid had quit, the fire insurance had been canceled and the engine in the Corvette had seized on the Ventura Freeway. The Chevrolet agency refused to honor the warranty on the Corvette and so she had called Detroit and told the head of public relations at General Motors that if the warranty was not honored she was going to drive the car to Detroit and burn the motherfucker on the lawn of John Z. DeLorean, vice-president and general manager of the Chevrolet division of General Motors. The head of public relations had suggested she see a psychiatrist. "What's new with you?" she said. (147)

The ambience of Las Vegas is so unselfconsciously bizarre and tawdry that sharp-eyed reporting is sufficient to take us to the very edge of surrealism. Although Dunne has invented several composite characters, manufactured some dialogue, and rearranged some scenes, his book has enough of an autobiographical flavor, complete with memories of childhood, to be taken pretty much at face value. During his stay in Vegas Dunne meets Maisy Morgan, a former show girl in the line at the Tropicana who, after her mastectomy, becomes a professional graphologist; a one-legged landlady named Dora whose ex-husband Harry Hyams used to get turned on sexually every time she would remove her artificial limb; and a private investigator named Buster Mano who was a student of the works of Martin Luther because both he and the great Reformer suffered from constipation. At the same time, Dunne learns that federal civil rights officials are considering a public accommodations complaint against a whorehouse eight miles east of Reno that refused to cater to black customers; that it is legal to send a stool sample, but not a dirty book, through the mail; and that a guy in Gary, Indiana, calls his member Jane, after *Jane's Fighting Ships*.

One is surprised that for a book as racy as *Vegas*, there are no lurid sex scenes. The dirt is all in the talk and in the imagination. After Dunne's youthful fantasies about movie sirens of the forties, he had graduated to voyeurism in his early adulthood. He particularly remembers one young lovely who lived across the street from him in New York. Nearly six feet tall, blond, and well-proportioned, she would come home in the afternoon, open the window, turn the stereo on loud, make herself a drink, take off her clothes, "and then stark naked, using her drink as a baton, . . . conduct Mozart's Concerto #5 in A-Major" (168). On one occasion he noticed that the girl's sexual partner was a classmate of his at Princeton. While in Vegas the closest that he comes to manifesting overt sexual desire—or so we are led to believe—is when he learns that his friend, comedian Jackie Kasey, is to be photographed with Miss Nevada. As it turns out, the beauty in question is not Miss Nevada but "a vapid teenager . . . with bangs and a Dust Bowl face, . . . wearing a black mini and high white vinyl boots and over her white nylon tricot blouse . . . a piece of cheap pink ribbon on which was printed, in gold letters, JR. MISS F.O.P.A., LODGE NO. 1" (196).

The comedian Jackie Kasey, one of Dunne's composite figures, is among the principal characters in the book. He is the sort of guy who will walk up to a troop of visiting girl scouts and say "I don't want no cookies" (56-57); who will ask the hotel intercom to page Kitty Litter and (say it real fast) Mike Hunt; and whose idea of ethnic humor is to say that the three times an Italian sees his priest are: "When he's baptized, when he's married and when they strap him into the electric chair" (188). He makes $10,000 a week but is still an opening act without big name appeal. He came up through the ranks playing mob-owned clubs in tank towns around the Midwest and spending his summers as "social director" in resorts for the sexually deprived. Nearly a decade later he will make an encore appearance as Las Vegas comedian Jackie Gross in *Dutch Shea, Jr.*

In one episode, Kasey is scheduled to appear with a whole lineup of superstars—Totie Fields, Tom Jones, Frank Gorshin, et al.—at a benefit for the Cancer Society. Unfortunately, when he arrives at the Flamingo, the only superstar who is there is Tanya the elephant. "There were a lot of kids in the audience and they were throwing peanuts at Tanya and Jackie Kasey felt as useless as a singer in a tit show" (231). Although he suggests that it might be best for him to wait until Tanya gets off before he goes on, the MC assures Jackie that it would be a funny bit for him to perform with the elephant. As he tries to adjust the microphone, Jackie is hit in the chest with a peanut aimed at Tanya. He then proceeds to dance around the stage, dodging Tanya's trunk and peanuts from the crowd, while singing "Bye Bye, Blackbird," and improvising nonsense syllables when he forgets the lyrics. When Jackie finally gets offstage, an acquaintance who is into social satire asks him what he thinks of Lenny Bruce and Dick Gregory. "Maybe the *schwartze* could work with Tanya, Jackie Kasey said, they both come out of the same goddam jungle" (232).

Another composite figure who appears sporadically throughout the pages of *Vegas* is the prostitute Artha Ging. She had taken accounting in high school in Milwaukee and now records statistics on her professional activities in a looseleaf notebook with a green-ink Parker 51 fountain pen. We learn that she has turned 1,203 tricks with 1,076 different johns and that these have included a wide variety of imaginative sexual practices. "Her vagina had been successfully penetrated by penises, dildos, bottles, bananas, frankfurters, candles and vibrators, and unsuccessfully by a pop-top can of Fresca" (30-31). Although she is studying to be a beautician, she has no intention of giving up her primary vocation, and takes a kind of perverse delight in the thought of servicing a woman's hair by day and more private parts of her husband's anatomy by night. She is also a poet:

> *Star light,*
> *Moon bright,*
> *Will I save my life tonight?*
> *In the stillness of the morn*
> *The question is,*
> *Why was I born?* (33)

The poetry was written by Joan Didion.

Vegas may not have sold well, but it was the turning point in Dunne's career. It enhanced his narrative range by doing two seemingly opposite, but actually complementary, things: it extended his imagination by taking him at least to the city limits of fiction, and it forced him deeper into himself by drawing upon personal experience—with her keen editorial eye, Didion kept advising him to "go back to the 'I' character." According to Dunne's own testimony: "*Vegas* was the book that made me realize that I could write about Irish Catholics" (Kasindorf 17). This realization paid off handsomely in his first "real" novel, *True Confessions*, a popular and critical success which reads as if it were written by a combination of Raymond Chandler, Charles Dickens, Brendan Behan, and Graham Greene. If there is one character who serves as a bridge from *Vegas* to *True Confessions*, it is the private investigator Buster Mano—Los Angeles Police Lieutenant Tom Spellacy in the later book—a lapsed Catholic whose wife was on familiar terms with the saints: " 'As I said to Jack this morning,' she would say; Jack was St. John Bosco and Frank was St. Francis de Sales. Her current litany was dedicated to 'the Babe,' which was her sobriquet for the Infant of Prague" (35).

True Confessions—a rich and complex novel to which some critics have reacted as Queen Victoria did to a three-hour Good Friday service, finding it to be altogether too much of a good thing—can be approached in a variety of ways. At one level, it represents the continuing appeal of the urban wild west of Hammett and Chandler. From another perspective, it may be one of the most consistently funny novels ever written, combining broad and bawdy humor with a dazzling number of "inside jokes" either ignored or missed by most critics. What is perhaps most impressive about *True Confessions*, however, is the integrity of its vision. The genuine entertainment that this novel offers is redeemed from gratuitousness by a world view that is theologically as well as culturally Catholic. Lapsed son of the Church though he is, Dunne writes with an Augustinian sense of sin and redemption.

It seems to me that *True Confessions* belongs to the tradition of Catholic modernism begun in the nineteenth century by Barbey d'Aurevilly and continued in our own time by such writers as Francois Mauriac, Evelyn Waugh, Muriel Spark, Flannery O'Connor, J.F. Powers, and Graham Greene. Collectively, these writers articulate what can be regarded as an "anti-humanist sensibility." In their novels, Martin Green points out, "human achievements and modes of being are consistently and triumphantly shown to be inadequate, egotistic, evil, just in being themselves, in being human. Under stress all natural goodness breaks down; only grace-assisted goodness is valid, and grace-assisted badness is perhaps even better" (*Blessing* 74). In one sense, then, the modern Catholic novel is almost indistinguishable from secular naturalistic fiction. But, as John B. Vickery so cogently argues, an anti-humanist bias is not itself sufficient to define a theological aesthetic (see "Secularity and Grace"). What also is needed is a fictively adequate means of depicting redemptive, *superhuman* grace. However, because such a depiction must be rendered in terms intelligible to a fallen world—which is to say, sacramentally—the Catholic novelist, like his secular counterpart, must begin by recognizing the world for the sinful place it is.

The world of *True Confessions* is one in which violence, lust, cupidity, deception, and sacrilege seem not only to endure but to prevail. The principal characters in this novel are Los Angeles Police Lieutenant Tom Spellacy and his brother Monsignor Desmond Spellacy. In the process of investigating the murder of a prostitute named Lois Fazenda, Tom uncovers lines of corruption that link the ecclesiastical and the secular realm at an astonishing number of points. The operative norm in both realms is a cynical worldly wisdom, and Dunne's most sagacious characters—clerical as well as lay—are in on the fix.

Among the clergy in the novel, there is a kind of hierarchy of sin: those at the lower ranks are guilty of more corporeal transgressions, while their superiors commit the higher, spiritual crimes. In the former category we find Tom Spellacy's daughter Moira, a 200-pound nun: "Moira is Sister Angelina now. A perfect name. Short for angel-food cake" (12). Then, there is the avaricious Monsignor McGrath, who almost excommunicates an automobile dealer when he fails to get an Oldsmobile Hydra-matic for his fiftieth birthday. Nowhere is the triumph of the flesh over the spirit more apparent, however, than in the case of Father Mickey Gagnon. "A real pain in the ass in confession" (99), who would give a penitent a rosary for picking his nose, Father Gagnon dies in the midst of a "heart-attack hump" while having "his ashes hauled" at a bordello.

In contrast, His Eminence Hugh Cardinal Danaher is above such temptations, and is even ascetic enough to celebrate a five A.M. Mass every day for sixty years. A wiley manipulator and ruthless autocrat, Danaher finds his greatest fulfillment in the quest for power. In the process, he uses his chancellor—the ambitious Des Spellacy—as "a combination lightning rod, hatchet man and accountant" (49). For his own part, Des is not above gaining political advantage through questionable means. He fixes a church raffle and writes a recommendation to Fordham for the delinquent son of an influential businessman. Also, he and the Cardinal both deal openly with Jack Amsterdam, a building contractor whose underworld connections are common knowledge. In one of his more introspective moments Des thinks his brother wrong to regard "the impulses of the flesh" as "the darkest sins .... Those impulses could be sublimated .... Hubris was the constant" (191).

Dunne, however, is no secular humanist engaging in anti-clerical satire; for his lay characters are depicted no more favorably than are their priestly counterparts. Generally corrupt and self-serving, they rarely show nobler instincts. And when they do, such instincts are usually undercut with brutal or obscene humor. For example, we have policeman Jerry Troy's efforts to console a lesbian who "sliced up her girlfriend ... , then tried to flush her down the toilet." "There she is telling Jerry how she couldn't fit the head down the crapper and she begins to cry. Really bawl. 'There, there,'

Jerry says. With that brogue you could cut. 'There, there, it's the sort of thing that could happen to any one of us' " (70-71).

With admirable metaphorical economy, Dunne concretely depicts the shared depravity of Church and World in the principal image of his novel—the dismembered body of Lois Fazenda. A votive candle having been inserted in her vagina, Miss Fazenda is oxymoronically dubbed "the Virgin Tramp." Moreover, her upper pubic region is decorated with the richly suggestive tattoo of a rose. Iconographically, the rose is a complex symbol drawing together a wealth of both sacred and secular connotations. For pagan culture it stood for "love triumphant; joy; beauty, desire . . . , an emblem of AphroditeVenus." For Christians, it has always been a representation of "heavenly bliss and the Virgin Mary as the Rose of Heaven" (Cooper 142), particularly in the cathedral at Chartres and in the final vision of Dante's *Divine Comedy*.

It might strike some as gratuitously perverse to find any religious affirmation in a novel as bawdy and blasphemous as *True Confessions*. However, as D. Keith Mano notes: "For any serious Christian writer the obscene, the grotesque, the violent seem almost prerequisite" ("Reflections" 5). This is because such a writer finds it extremely difficult to convey the awesomeness of faith to an audience "which—more likely than not—doesn't share the powerful sign language by which Christians communicate in shorthand with one another: the Cross, the Trinity, sacraments, Grace. And that enormous paradox: death into life" (5). "In a profane age," Mano concludes, "the profane must be taken unawares and in their own tongue" (10).

Of course, even if one agrees with this rather venturesome position, it does not follow that everything obscene is necessarily covert theology. What is crucial is the use to which obscenity is put. As an extension of the anti-humanist sensibility of modern Catholic fiction, the obscene helps to accentuate the fallenness of the world. In confronting that fallenness the reader is left with essentially two choices: either retreat into cynicism and despair or find deliverance from those emotions through the agency of grace. And for all its surface nihilism, the central story of *True Confessions* depicts the latter course. Dunne's novel, like J.F. Powers's *Morte D'Urban*, is fundamentally the spiritual drama of a priest who—through a series of ostensible misfortunes—recovers his true vocation.

Although time-present in this novel is the mid-seventies, the murder of Lois Fazenda occurs in the late 1940s. The bulk of the story consists of flashbacks related from a selectively omniscient third-person point of view. The focus of these flashbacks alternates between the consciousness of Tom and that of Des, with some very brief glimpses into the minds of Cardinal Danaher and Tom's mistress Corinne. However, *True Confessions* opens and closes with first-person present-time narrations from the viewpoint of Tom Spellacy. On balance, then, Tom's perspective is the center of consciousness in Dunne's novel. But since Tom can hardly be considered a moral norm, we must look beyond his sensibility and read between the lines of his narration to appreciate fully his brother's spiritual regeneration.

At the beginning of *True Confessions* an aging Tom Spellacy visits his brother Des, who for the past twenty-eight years has been pastor of a small desert parish. Upon arriving at the rectory Tom meets his brother's curate, Father Eduardo, who refers to Des as "a totally dedicated priest . . . a real Catholic of the old school" (19). Later, Des tells Tom about the mundane activities of a parish priest; and when his brother asks "How are you, Des," the monsignor replies: "I'm going to die, Tommy" (22).

During his days as chancellor of the archdiocese, Des had been an upwardly mobile priest—clearly destined for a bishop's mitre, if not the red hat of a cardinal. Like Powers's Father Urban, he had made friends with the mammon of unrighteousness in order to advance the Church's—and his own—worldly interests. And unlike the novel's more conventionally pious characters, who are blinded to reality by either insanity or stupidity, Des knows the world as it is. Cardinal Danaher reflects that his chancellor "accepted as a given the taint on the human condition" (112). "A little humanity was the only thing the monsignor seemed deficient in" (111).

One character in the novel consistently represents a golden mean between the cynical opportunism of Des and Cardinal Danaher and the ineffectual religiosity of such figures as Tom's mentally ill wife Mary Margaret. He is Monsignor Seamus Fargo. Like Hugh Danaher, Seamus is an eighty-year-old priest; but unlike the Cardinal, Monsignor Fargo is a man of "flinty intractability." Both men had been curates in Boston before the turn of the century; and, perhaps for that reason, Seamus "was the only priest in the archdiocese who could crack the Cardinal's composure" (124).

A crotchety old prelate with his share of intellectual and ethnic prejudices, Seamus Fargo is nevertheless a man of intelligence, compassion, and biting candor. As a result, he was exiled early in his career from Boston to Los Angeles for running afoul of a high-living cardinal. As Hugh Danaher tells the story:

> Every winter Cardinal Sheehan would go to Nassau. When the frost was on the pumpkin, so to speak, there would be the Cardinal sailing out of Boston harbor, giving his blessing .... "Isn't it grand?" the old biddies in the archdiocese would say. They didn't have two lumps of coal to see them through the winter .... "Ah, yes," Seamus would say. "Such a sensitive man, His Eminence. You know why he goes to Nassau, don't you? It just

breaks his heart to see the poor shiver in the dead
of winter." (124-25)

When Des Spellacy was coming up through the clerical ranks, he
had served as curate in Monsignor Fargo's parish. Although his
feelings are not reciprocated, Des likes and respects Seamus and
maintains him as his confessor. By depicting Des as an ambivalent
and troubled man who is periodically confronted with the moral
alternative of Seamus's lifestyle, Dunne goes a long way toward
making Des's eventual adoption of that lifestyle psychologically
credible.

The external action that resolves the plot of *True Confessions*
appropriately brings together the novel's secular and ecclesiastical
subplots. When Jack Amsterdam's moral callousness results in the
suicide of Tom Spellacy's old girlfriend Brenda, Tom decides to
bring Jack in for questioning in the Lois Fazenda case. By this
point in the story Tom knows that Amsterdam is innocent of that
particular crime, but he believes that some police harassment of
Jack would be at least partial retribution for Brenda's death.
Although he dies of throat cancer before being indicted or cleared,
Jack Amsterdam reveals enough about his dealings with the Church
to ruin Des's chance of ever becoming a more exalted "bookkeeper
in ermine." His ecclesiastical career in shambles, Monsignor Spellacy
asks the Cardinal to assign him as curate to Seamus Fargo in
the desert parish to which Seamus has been exiled. In an ironic
twist on the Cain and Abel story, Tom Spellacy has set in motion
a chain of events that destroys his brother's ecclesiastical ambitions.

In addition to an anti-humanist moral vision, *True Confessions*
articulates an anti-rationalist epistemology. Unlike his officious
superior on the police force, Tom does not believe in the "systems
approach" to crime detection. Instead, after having lived for so

34

many years with a fruitcake wife, he appreciates the randomness of the human psyche. As in Roman Polanski's *Chinatown*, the central crime in Dunne's novel finally has nothing to do with the elaborate web of public corruption that is exposed in the investigation of that crime, but with a totally unrelated private compulsion. The world of this novel, then, is not that of an ordered Thomistic universe. In another context Des observes: "I was always the one who connected the lines before. Not now. The pencil had a power of its own. No one had any control over it" (261).

If God acts in such a world, it is frequently through arbitrary circumstance. For example, in what appears to be one of the more farcical images of the novel, we find an ironic evocation of the Paraclete. When Des serves as a chaplain during World War II, he parachutes from an airplane into a minefield with an altar stone and twenty-four thousand communion wafers. In the course of his descent, the hosts are ripped from his arm and scattered over the battlefield. He lands among the German mines with a broken altar stone, while the visible symbol of God's presence falls "like snow" upon the enemy. Similarly, in the main plot of *True Confessions*, God's grace enters the world despite the seeming fragmentation and collapse of the institutional Church.

What really holds the disparate pieces of this novel together is the relationship between the Spellacy brothers. Although Tom is certainly not a moral foil like Seamus Fargo, he helps to keep Des honest in other ways. Because Tom can see through his brother's dissimulations and those of the Church, his encounters with Des force the monsignor to reveal more than a few of his own sins. If he is not exactly a penitent, Des is at least stripped of some of his smugness. As the paperback blurb notes, Dunne's novel is about two brothers "in the confession business."

Returning to time-present for the conclusion of the novel, we witness the final meeting of the Spellacy brothers, an encounter that is itself a kind of confession: "I suppose Des bringing me out to the desert was his way of giving me absolution" (337), Tom tells us. After informing his brother of his own impending death, Des speaks of Seamus Fargo: "He taught me how to be a priest, Tommy. I have no gift for loving God. I still don't. Seamus said that wasn't a drawback, as long as I could be useful, and out here in this Godforsaken place, I am useful .... There's a kind of peace in that, Tommy. I can't help it if you don't believe it, but it's true" (339). Filled with remorse, Tom declares: "I'm sorry, Des .... It was my fault." But Des holds up his hand, as if in benediction, and replies: "You were my salvation, Tommy" (340).

Absolution has been given, and the peace has been passed between the two brothers. Referring to himself and Tom in the ethnic slang of their childhood, Desmond says: "You made me remember something I forgot. Or tried to forget is more like it. You and me, we were always just a couple of harps" (340). In this statement Des may be asserting more than mere genetic or even racial kinship. Perhaps he is saying, with the author of the Book of Job, that every man is "a brother to dragons and a companion to owls," that our brotherhood is defined by a shared patrimony of Original Sin. In a sense, Des's epiphany is not entirely dissimilar to what the grandmother experiences just prior to her death in Flannery O'Connor's "A Good Man Is Hard to Find." Confronting a psychopathic killer called The Misfit, she exclaims: "Why, you're one of my babies. You're one of my own children!" (*Stories* 132).

Just as the title *True Confessions* suggests a kind of tabloid sensationalism, so too is much of Dunne's novel concerned with the violent and sordid aspects of life. Yet, when one gets beyond its grotesquely naturalistic depiction of Hammett-Chandler country and beyond the murder mystery that is the ostensible focus of its plot, one sees that this novel deals with a higher truth and a higher confession. Tom Spellacy can give us a recitation of facts with all the objectivity of a police report. His brother, however, has discovered a truth that transcends the recitation of mere facts. Ultimately, Des's story is closer to the *Confessions of Saint Augustine* than it is to the tawdry revelations of pulp journalism. Rather than "living out his death," he dies into Life. And in the process, he experiences what Graham Greene once called the "appalling strangeness" of God's mercy.

Although reasonable people may disagree about the place of *True Confessions* within the canon of Catholic modernism, no one can deny its surface affinities with a host of recent novels that exploit pre-Vatican II Catholic nostalgia. For the most part, these novels are written by lapsed Catholics who are far enough removed from the days of the Latin Mass and fish on Friday to regard those halcyon times with the affection reserved for memories of old school ties that no longer bind. Joining Dunne in this class of Catholic alumni are novelists such as Elizabeth Cullinan, in *House of Gold*; William Gibson, in *A Mass for the Dead*; and—preeminently—Mary Gordon, in *Final Payments* and *The Company of Women*. What we detect in their writing is a kind of elegiac consciousness not unlike that which pervaded the literature of the Southern Renaissance. As Garry Wills has observed: "Winners erect their own monuments, while losers ache with music" (*Choirs* 5).

In his 1982 novel, *Dutch Shea, Jr.*, Dunne exploits some of the same devices that made *True Confessions* so entertaining—off-beat characters, bawdy humor, intricate plotting, authentic dialogue, and Irish-Catholic ethnicity. The *cognoscenti* will even note that Dunne once again uses the name "Harold Pugh": in *Vegas* Harold is a salesman of patio furniture who has skipped out on a gambling debt; in *True Confessions* he is a kinky barber who proves to be the key in the Lois Fazenda murder case; and in *Dutch Shea, Jr.* he is simply a corpse laid out in a funeral home. The most important thread linking these two novels, however, is Dunne's ambivalent attitude toward his own past. That this ambivalence is reflected in terms of both time and place is suggested by an epigraph and a note preceding the text of *Dutch Shea, Jr.* The epigraph (from Evelyn Waugh's *Brideshead Revisited*) reads, "for we possess nothing certainly except the past." The note tells us that the setting of the novel is "in equal parts the city where I spent the first eighteen years of my life and the city where I have lived the last seventeen." To a somewhat less obvious extent, both of these generalizations also apply to *True Confessions*.

Although such things are difficult to assess, it is probable that a personal tragedy that occurred while Dunne was working on *Dutch Shea* deeply influenced the novel. In the 7 April 1980 issue of *New West*, Dunne tells of being awakened at 4:30 in the morning by a phone call informing him that his younger brother Stephen, age 43, had committed suicide. This experience caused Dunne to meditate more deeply on the meaning of suicide, which plays a crucial role in his novel, and on the significance of his own roots. In one key passage of his *New West* piece he tells us of a "photograph of Stephen, an infant, held in the lap of his grandfather Burns . . . . , [whose] first job, as a child not yet ten, was handing out Civil War casualty lists, the endless wounded and dead from Second Manassas and Fredericksburg. There in that one photograph of the old man and the infant is a family continuum from the Famine through Antietam and Bull Run to the hot and cold wars and police actions and social dislocations of our own time" (91). Appropriately, the dedication of *Dutch Shea, Jr.* reads: "This book is for my grandfather / Dominick Francis Burns / and for my beloved brother / Stephen Burns Dunne / May they rest in peace."

In his memorial to Stephen, Dunne quotes a passage from Gerard Manley Hopkins which later shows up as another epigraph to his novel:

> O the mind, mind has mountains; cliffs of fall
> Frightful, sheer, no-man fathomed. Hold them cheap
> May who ne'er hung there ....
>
> I wake and feel the fell of dark, not day.

There is, nevertheless, a ray of hope in the *New West* article that is absent from *Dutch Shea, Jr.* Here, Dunne recalls other lines from Hopkins: "*I have desired to go / Where springs not fail, / To fields where flies no sharp and sided hail / And a few lilies blow.*"

He then concludes:

> I remember spending Christmas in Hartford a couple of years ago. An acquaintance of the family had committed suicide the day after Christmas. Ever the optimist, our aunt said, "Well, at least he didn't ruin their Christmas." Stephen looked at me, a cigarette burning his finger, a smile softening the corner of his face. "No," he said, "but it sure tore the shit out of their December 26th." I think of Stephen and I know there will be a small piece torn out of every day for the rest of my days. I will not ask why. I hold his mountains dear. I hope he is where the lilies blow. (92)

Although the geographical setting of *True Confessions* and *Dutch Shea, Jr.* is a composite of Hartford and Los Angeles, the moral landscape of both novels involves a juxtaposition of unassimilated Irish Catholicism with big-city venality and corruption. In the latter novel the bridge between these two worlds is Dunne's title character—a seedy pimp lawyer who, like Paul Newman in *The Verdict*, hides his instinctive sentimentality behind a self-protective cynicism. Dutch Shea, Jr., is a scoundrel who speculates with the life savings of a nursing home patient whose estate is entrusted to his care. However, he loved his convict father, a jailhouse suicide, and his adopted daughter, killed by a terrorist bomb; and he seems to be as much the victim as the master of the women who share his bed—specifically an estranged Episcopalian wife, a tough criminal-court judge, and the wealthy widow of the man who cuckolded him.

Like *True Confessions, Dutch Shea, Jr.* is a feast of ethnic, sexual, and scatological humor. Dunne's Irish-American characters share rather predictable views about "Polacks," "fags," "spics," "coloreds," and other exotic types. Among the more memorable characters to pass through Dutch Shea's world are a black heroin addict who breaks into his apartment (remember the scene in Saul Bellow's *Mr. Sammler's Planet* where a swaggering Harlemite exposes himself to the beleaguered Jewish professor; well, Dunne goes Bellow one better by having his dusky intruder spill his seed into the picture of a shapely blonde who turns out to be an undercover cop); a Puerto Rican pyromaniac who is acquitted of an arson charge when it is proved that at the time of the fire he was fellating a prominent judge (a phallic birthmark blows the judge's cover); and Packy Considine, the dumbest client Dutch had ever represented.

Packy was "wheelman in an armored car stickup. His first mistake. The second mistake was the take. One hundred seventy-six thousand dollars. Except it was in nonnegotiable bonds. Plus twenty-nine dollars cash. All of it in pennies. Mistake number three was the getaway car. Stolen by Packy. A Ford Galaxie. Innocuous enough. Except for the bumper sticker that said, I'VE GOT MY SHIT TOGETHER BUT NOW I CAN'T PICK IT UP. Three armored car guards and seventeen eyewitnesses remembered the bumper sticker. It made for a difficult defense" (58).

Dutch Shea, Jr. is likely to strike those who are unfamiliar with Dunne's previous work as a particularly engaging and entertaining novel. Those who have read the other books will still find much to admire in this one, but will also feel a twinge of *déjà vu*. John "Dutch" Shea may not be John Gregory Dunne, but both are Irish-American Catholics with Episcopalian wives and adopted daughters. While traveling west on a plane late in the novel, Dutch refuses to pull down his window shade so that the other passengers can see the movie. His explanation: "I just want to look out the window. I don't want to watch Barbra Streisand taking a bath with Kris Kristofferson" (365). At another point Dunne has Father Hugh Campion remark that a priest in seminary had told him that the "difference between moral and venial sin varied from parish to parish" (272). This is precisely what a priest told Joan Didion when, in the early sixties, she was contemplating "marrying outside her faith," as such unions were then characterized. And perhaps most obvious is the reincarnation of Jackie Kasey from *Vegas* as Jackie Gross—*née* Grossbart—in *Dutch Shea*. The only new wrinkle is an answering service that proclaims: "At the sound of the beep, kiss my ass" (371). Which is at least an improvement over "Have a nice day."

Because Dunne is a gifted narrative craftsman, his story and his protagonist become more interesting as the novel progresses. The "Jr." in Dutch Shea's name suggests the importance of his past. Dutch has spent much of his life trying to cope with ambivalent feelings about his father. He loves him; but he also feels shame at being the son of an embezzler who hanged himself in his prison cell. In one of the novel's many ironic reversals, Dutch learns that his father had actually taken the rap for a friend—the upright businessman D. F. Campion. Although D. F. becomes foster father to Dutch and raises him in the shadow of a portrait of Pius XII, he had willingly allowed Dutch, Sr., to serve as his scapegoat.

If Dutch, Jr., is troubled by his roots, his later family life proves equally problematic. His wife Lee is a cold, aristocratic woman who has been made infertile by a venereal disease that she contracted at college. Their mutual infidelities finally lead to divorce and to Dutch's own self-destructive apathy. With his wife gone, the two main women in his life are a wealthy Catholic widow whom he can't stand and a judge whose career would be ruined by public association with a skid-row attorney. The only person whom Dutch ever loved selflessly and without reservation was his adopted daughter Catherine, and she is dead.

Employing a novelistic trope at least as old as Henry Fielding, Dunne makes the issue of Catherine's parentage crucial to his denouement. When he discovers that a maid in D. F. Campion's home had given birth to an illegitimate child shortly before his adoption of Catherine, Dutch travels to Las Vegas in search of that maid, who when last heard of was one of Jackie Gross's mistresses. Although it would be unfair to reveal Dunne's surprise ending, I will say that what Dutch learns in Las Vegas helps him to understand things that he might have preferred never to have known.

Despite Dunne's obvious skill as a humorist and storyteller, *Dutch Shea, Jr.* is not an entirely successful novel. So much of its ambience is derived from *True Confessions* that Dunne reminds one of a nightclub comic who recycles many of the same jokes performance after performance—Philip Roth and other ethnic realists appear to have fallen into much the same rut. Also, there are points where the novel's tawdriness and sensationalism seem forced to the point of self-consciousness. At times—as in his depiction of a hapless black woman who accidentally runs over her baby granddaughter with a power lawn mower—Dunne even crosses the thin line between absurd humor and gratuitous cruelty. Tact and discretion are not among this novel's many virtues.

Ultimately, the moral vision of *Dutch Shea, Jr.* is bleaker than that of *True Confessions.* In Dunne's earlier novel the corruption of the world caused a priest to recover his vocation; however, that same corruption only plunges Dutch Shea deeper into the Slough of Despond. Dutch experiences the dark night of the soul without ever glimpsing the dawn that Dunne is able to imagine for his brother Stephen. And deprived of grace, the world is not only a harrowing jungle, but also a crashing bore. Dunne's limited achievement in *Dutch Shea, Jr.* is the result more of artifice than of conviction.

As important as his Frog Hollow roots might be, Dunne uses the Irish Catholic ghetto of Hartford as only part of the symbolic landscape of his two novels and as the dominant ambience of only one of the sections of the autobiographical *Vegas.* A far more pervasive concern of his writing is his identity as a naturalized citizen of the New West. Indeed, he has entitled the final section of *Quintana & Friends* "Continental Drift," after a geologist's term which, Dunne tells us, is "defined in the *Random House Dictionary of the English Language* as 'the hypothetical tendency or ability of continents to drift on the earth's surface because of the weakness of the suboceanic crust.' " "I come from generations in the East," he continues, "I have settled in the West, and if there is a single thread in this book it is the confrontation of the transplanted Easterner with the culture of the contemporary West" (xvii). Dunne's more or less definitive statement on this confrontation comes in the culminating essay of this collection—a regionalist *apologia* called "Eureka."

Dunne begins by distinguishing the sociological forces that led to the settling of Los Angeles from those that shaped the history of northern California. Relying on the writings of Carey McWilliams and on his own shrewd insights, Dunne demonstrates how present-day Los Angeles is a logical outgrowth of its own unique past. The nineteenth-century migration to Los Angeles, he notes, was a phenomenon that "seemed to parody Frederick Jackson Turner and his theory on the significance of the frontier" (253). Although northern California was settled by the hardy pioneers who best exemplify the Turner thesis, Los Angeles was never the destination of those who crossed the American wilderness in Conestoga wagons. The settlers of Los Angeles may have traversed much of the same terrain as their counterparts to the north, but their trek was made on "an excursion ticket." When the Santa Fe Railroad laid its track into southern California in 1886, a rate war ensued which finally led on 6 March 1887 to a fare of one dollar per passenger from the Missouri Valley to the west coast.

"What the railroads had essentially created in southern California," Dunne writes, "was a frontier resort, a tumor on the western ethic. Bargain basement pioneers, everyone a rebuke to Turner's hard man, flooded into southern California .... If New York was the melting pot of Europe, Los Angeles was the melting pot of the United States" (254). While the Central Valley and other areas to the north were developing a relatively stable agrarian society, southern California increasingly became a region of aliens and the con men who preyed on them. In the first four decades of this century, the population of Los Angeles grew by 1,600 percent.

With the arrival of all these migrants, many of whom were attempting to sever their ties with the past, it was inevitable that southern California develop an ad hoc culture in which the very idea of community was anachronistic. In addition, the spectacular growth of Los Angeles exactly coincided with the automotive age and its ethic of personal autonomy. "Los Angeles," Dunne observes, "was the first city on wheels, its landscape in three directions unbroken by natural barriers that could give it coherence and definition, its mobility limited only by a tank of gas" (255).

Nevertheless, until World War II it was possible for the rest of America to dismiss southern California as "a sunstroked curiosity, . . . a provincial and distant colony" (255). Despite its abundance of technological know-how, Los Angeles had no industrial base. Not only was its non-agricultural economy service-oriented, but the linchpin of that economy—Hollywood—required no raw materials except for celluloid. Producing very little in the way of tangible commodities, the motion picture industry—in 1938—nevertheless ranked fourteenth among all American businesses in gross volume and eleventh in total assets.

Then came the Second World War and the transformation of southern California from a west-coast anomaly into one of the nation's principal industrial centers. In Los Angeles there was no conversion to wartime production, but rather the emergence of an entirely new technological infrastructure. Unhampered by the industrial obsolescence and geographical constraints that plagued the East and the Midwest, southern California blossomed into a boomtown region whose indigenous metals and chemicals and wide-open spaces seemed providentially designed for the construction and testing of democracy's arsenal.

Among other things, wartime prosperity allowed southern California to forge a kind of civic identity. Speaking of that identity, J. D. Lorenz writes: "In a land without roots, reality was image, image replaced roots, and if the image could be constructed quickly, like a fabricated house, it could also be torn down quickly" (see *Quintana* 257). Rather than contradict this assessment, Dunne contends that Los Angeles is unashamedly, even enthusiastically, the way Lorenz describes it: "Better the fresh start than roots choking with moral crab grass, better the fabricated house than the dry rot of cities, better mind over matter than a paralysis of will" (257).

If the strident individualism of southern California is largely a product of historical and geographical forces rather than conscious design, the inhabitants of that region soon came to regard their independent lifestyle as a feisty rebuke to the clannish east coast. "See what community got you, it seemed to say; what good are stability and cohesion if their legacy is the South Bronx?" (257). The post-World War II years saw millions of Americans succumb to this logic as the excursion-ticket immigration to Los Angeles continued. It was a trip that John Gregory Dunne himself made in 1964, a half dozen years after his beloved Dodgers.

One of the themes that runs through Dunne's essay is that of the antithesis of Los Angeles and New York. Having lived in both places, Dunne is perhaps overly sensitive to the differences between these two major cities. However, their battle for cultural supremacy has implications that extend beyond his personal frame of reference. As he notes: "The history of nationhood is also largely the history of a nation's single city—that London, that Paris, that New York (with Washington as its outermost exurb) where politics, money and culture coalesce to shape a national idea. Every place else is a Manchester or Marseilles" (257). The claim of Los Angeles to be our nation's major city—the equal of New York—lies in its near monopoly of the image media of motion pictures and television.

Defining a useful—if overly neat—dichotomy, Dunne sees a war being waged between the opinion media of the East and the image media of the West for the hearts and minds of America.

Ultimately, then, it is not the difference between a subway and freeway mentality that most profoundly separates New York from Los Angeles. Whether one loves or loathes southern California finally depends on one's attitude toward the motion picture industry. As Dunne notes: "This country has always been defined by the East. Everything was good or bad to the extent that it did or did not coincide with the eastern norm; the making of cultural rules, the fact of being the nation's social and cultural arbiter, imbued confidence. The movies were a severe shock to that confidence, all the more so because those images up there on screen did not seem to have an apparent editorial bias" (259).

If Dunne's *paean* to Los Angeles smacks of highbrow civic boosterism, allowance probably should be made for a newcomer's enthusiasm. Dunne, after all, is a converted Easterner. A self-confessed "jerk" from Hartford by way of New York City, he found a kind of secular redemption in southern California. For him the image of that journey assumes a virtually beatific aura. "Fly west from the Atlantic seaboard," he writes, "see the country open up below, there some lights, over there a town, on the horizon perhaps a city, in between massive, implacable emptiness .... We have a sense out here, however specious, of being alone, of wanting, more importantly, to be left alone, of having our own space, a kingdom of self" (261).

Because—in a mythic sense—space and time tend to merge, Los Angeles can be viewed as a post-Eastern city. Paradoxically, however, it is also post-Western. The belief that our journey west was literally without end ceased with the closing of the American frontier, just as surely as it began with the discovery of the New World.

In the four centuries between Columbus in 1492 and Frederick Jackson Turner in 1893, the West was seen as a road rather than a barrier. But now that that road has ended at a barrier called the Pacific Ocean, present-day California has returned to the condition of medieval Europe in being a world without a West.

Thus, when we consider the radical solipsism and pervasive unreality of contemporary Los Angeles, it is perhaps useful to remember what Leslie Fiedler says of the European imagination prior to Columbus: "Excluded from geography and history, the West persisted as fantasy, legend, a place to be sought inside the skull of ordinary dreamers or inspired poets" (*Return* 30). In words that serve as Dunne's epigraph to *Quintana & Friends*, Theodore Roosevelt observed: "When I am in California, I am not in the West. I am west of the West."

To be a regionalist writer in America means more than merely coming from a certain part of the country. Otherwise, everyone would be a regionalist, and the term would have only a biographical— and no literary—significance. A regionalist, it seems to me, is one whose very impulse to write is largely shaped by his response to a particular locale. No doubt, William Faulkner would have been a great novelist even if he had not been born in the South, but the specific nature of his greatness would have been different. As Faulkner once said in Leslie Fiedler's presence, "To write about a place well, you must hate it! ... The way a man hates his wife" (*Essays*, 2: 333). If Dunne possesses this sort of loving hatred, it is not for California, but for his Irish-Catholic past. For him the New West is more a mistress than a wife.

Although Dunne may not have the particular gift to mythicize California, he at least has the integrity not to romanticize it as either the golden dream or the tinsel scam. Like a good mistress, El Lay has given Dunne pleasure without demanding commitment.

In return, he has tried to tell the unfashionable truth about his life west of the West. In *The Studio*, his Hollywood essays, and his own practice as a screenwriter, he has taken the novel approach of accepting Hollywood on its own terms. His attitude would seem to be that of Fitzgerald's Cecilia Brady: "You can take Hollywood for granted like I did, or you can dismiss it with the contempt we reserve for what we don't understand" (*Tycoon* 3). Just as he is now setting the standard for the Irish-Catholic novel, Dunne may one day revise the standard for the Hollywood novel. As he himself observed, yesterday's "schmucks with Underwoods" are today's "schmucks with word processors" ("Hessians" 34).

What makes Dunne, even when considered only as a Western or post-Western writer, infinitely more than an Irish Sammy Glick is his role in acquainting America with a non-Hollywood segment of California culture. He was, after all, the national journalist who "discovered" Cesar Chavez, a fact that John Lahr conveniently ignores in his mania to depict Dunne as a sunbelt hedonist devoid of a social conscience. And, as he reveals in the 16 August 1984 issue of the *New York Review of Books*, Dunne's interest in the Chicano community did not end with the grape strike in Delano. For nearly twenty years Didion and Dunne have been close friends of Dan and Lilith James. A blacklisted Communist screenwriter from Kansas City, Dan James has lived for many years among the Chicanos of East Los Angeles. A little over a decade ago he began publishing fiction under the name of "Danny Santiago," and his first collection of stories—*Famous All Over Town*—won the 1984 Rosenthal Award as an "American work of fiction published during the preceding twelve months which, though not a commercial success, is a considerable achievement."

In his long essay "The Secret of Danny Santiago," Dunne not only tells the story of Dan James, but also informs us of his own role in helping "Danny Santiago" get published. Although he is himself a Midwestern WASP, James apparently writes with sensitivity and understanding about the lives of Mexican Americans. In California the encounter between Anglo and Hispanic offers some of the same rich literary possibilities as do the relations between black and white in the South and Indian and white in the prairie states. Dunne may not have the necessary experience and sensibility to render this theme in fiction, but he is intelligent and humane enough to know that the Chicano story is one that needs to be told. *Delano* and "The Secret of Danny Santiago" are evidence of this perception. But then, Dunne knows something about the struggle of an ethnic Catholic minority to make it in American society.

At the end of "The Secret of Danny Santiago" Dunne writes:

> When we returned to Los Angeles, my wife and I drove down to Lamar Street in Lincoln Heights. The entire three blocks had been flattened to make a parking lot for the piggy-back trailers that ride the Southern Pacific flatcars. In [Santiago's] book, when the Southern Pacific succeeds in condemning the neighborhood, Chato Medina writes his name in Crayola on every flat surface in the area. It is the gesture that makes him "famous all over town." I had no Crayola in the car. If I had, I would have written four words on the sidewalk of Lamar Street: "Dan and Lilith James." (27)

Joan Didion and John Gregory Dunne have written their names large across the literature of the contemporary American West.

Selected Bibliography

WORKS CITED

Cooper, J. C. *An Illustrated Encyclopedia of Traditional Symbols*. London: Thames, 1978.

Dunne, John Gregory. "About Stephen." *New West* 7 Apr. 1980: 91-92.

_____ . *Delano: The Story of the California Grape Strike*. New York: Farrar, 1967.

_____ . *Dutch Shea, Jr.* New York: Linden-Simon, 1982. New York: Pocket, 1983.

_____ . "Hollywood Hessians" (review of *The Craft of the Screenwriter*, by John Brady). *New York Review of Books* 19 Nov. 1981: 34-37.

_____ . *Quintana & Friends*. New York: Dutton, 1978.

_____ . "The Secret of Danny Santiago" (review of *Famous All Over Town*, by Danny Santiago). *New York Review of Books* 16 Aug. 1984: 17-18, 20, 22, 24-27.

_____ . *The Studio*. New York: Farrar, 1969.

_____ . *True Confessions*. New York: Dutton, 1978.

_____ . *Vegas: A Memoir of a Dark Season*. 1974. New York: Warner, 1975.

Fiedler, Leslie A. *The Collected Essays of Leslie Fiedler*. 2 vols. New York: Stein, 1971.

_____ . *The Return of the Vanishing American*. New York: Stein, 1967.

Fitzgerald, F. Scott. *The Last Tycoon*. New York: Scribner's, 1941.

Green, Martin. *Yeats's Blessing on Von Hugel*. London: Longmans, 1967.

Kasindorf, Martin. "New Directions for the First Family of Angst." *Saturday Review* Apr. 1982: 14-18.

Lahr, John. "Entrepreneurs of Anxiety." *Horizon* Jan. 1981: 36, 38-39.

Mano, D. Keith. "Reflections of a Christian Pornographer." *Christianity and Literature* 28 (1979): 5-11.

O'Connor, Flannery. *The Complete Stories*. New York: Farrar, 1971.

Simon, John. *Paradigms Lost: Reflections on Literacy and Its Decline.* New York: Potter, 1980.

Vickery, John B. "J. F. Powers' *Morte D'Urban*: Secularity and Grace." *The Vision Obscured: Perceptions of Some Twentieth-Century Catholic Novelists.* Ed. Melvin J. Friedman. New York: Fordham UP, 1970. 45-65.

Wills, Garry. *Bare Ruined Choirs.* Garden City: Doubleday, 1972.

SELECTED PRIMARY WORKS NOT CITED

"Chinatowns" (review of *Water and Power*, by William L. Kahrl; and *The California Water Atlas*, ed. by William L. Kahrl). *New York Review of Books* 21 Oct. 1982: 6, 8, 10.

"Elephant Man" (review of *The Kennedy Imprisonment*, by Garry Wills). *New York Review of Books* 15 Apr. 1982: 10-13.

"Happy Days Are Here Again" (review of *Overdrive: A Personal Documentary*, by William F. Buckley, Jr.). *New York Review of Books* 13 Oct. 1983: 20, 28-30.

"Hog Heaven" (review of *The Right Stuff*, by Tom Wolfe). *New York Review of Books* 8 Nov. 1979: 9-12.

SELECTED CRITICISM

Adams, Robert M. "Shyster Saints." *New York Review of Books* 10 June 1982: 31-32. Largely favorable review of *Dutch Shea, Jr.*

Buckley, William F., Jr. "Hollywood Piety." *National Review* 18 Sept. 1981: 1091-93. Finds the film version of *True Confessions* vastly inferior to the novel.

Cook, Bruce. "Dark Season." *New Republic* 9 Mar. 1974: 28. Positive review of *Vegas.*

Duberman, Martin. "Grapes of Wrath." *New Republic* 2 Dec. 1967: 23-26. Mostly negative review of *Delano.*

Grenier, Richard. "Our Lady of Corruption." *Commentary* Dec. 1981: 79-83.

A rave review of the film *True Confessions.*

Kasindorf, Martin. "New Directions for the First Family of Angst." *Saturday Review* Apr. 1982: 14-18. A feature article on Didion and Dunne.

Lahr, John. "Entrepreneurs of Anxiety." *Horizon* Jan. 1981: 36, 38-39. A vitriolic attack on Didion and Dunne.

Mars-Jones, Adam. "Ugliest is Best." *Times Literary Supplement* 17 Sept. 1982: 992. Negative review of *Dutch Shea, Jr.*

Rascoe, Judith. "Sins of Omission." *Harper's* Nov. 1977: 106-08. An extremely favorable review of the novel *True Confessions.*

Richler, Mordecai. "I Hang Around." *New York Times Book Review* 28 Jan. 1979: 9, 27. Mixed review of *Quintana & Friends.*

Skenazy, Paul. "History as Mystery, or Who Killed L.A.?" *Los Angeles in Fiction: A Collection of Original Essays.* Ed. David Fine. Albuquerque: U of New Mexico P, 1984. 223-41. A discussion of the novel *True Confessions* and Thomas Sanchez's *The Zoot-Suit Murders.*

Stein, Benjamin. "L.A. Lace." *National Review* 9 Dec. 1977: 1440-41. Rave review of the novel *True Confessions.*

Yardley, Jonathan. "Reportage as Anesthesia." *New York Times Book Review* 3 Dec. 1974: 6-7. Generally positive review of *Vegas.*

Zimmerman, Paul D. "The Infernal Regions." *Newsweek* 12 May 1969: 110, 112, 114. A positive review of *The Studio.*

Date Due